D.R.E.S.S.E.D.
Demonstrating Readiness Equipping Saints for Service Every Day

PREPARED FOR EVERY GOOD WORK
Carolyn V. Kinard

table
OF CONTENTS

This book is dedicated to my amazing family, my husband Garland of 45 years. We have weathered many storms in our lives, but our love for each other has never wavered. God has been faithful to us. I love you with all my heart. To my adult children, Kenny; LaToya (Alvin); LeVar, and my granddaughter, Ananda. You are my greatest accomplishment. You are a precious gift from God. I am so proud to be your mother. Your wisdom, strength, endurance and accountability is refreshing to me in this day and time.

My siblings, Sherman Jr. (Pamala); Sharon (Charles); David; Rosalyn, and Gary (Dorea). All of my nieces and nephews and all of my great nieces and nephews. I love you so much. Our family tied is so strong. Your love has given me strength to continue this journey. I am grateful for the many prayers, words of wisdom, and fellowship. Continue to walk in excellence and fight the good fight of faith. "We are what we repeatedly do. Excellence, then, is not an act, but a habit." Aristotle

To the Churches all over the world that covered my family and I through *Watch Care for many years*, and to my home church, Emmanuel United Pentecostal Church, Camden, NJ; Thank you for the love shown to us and the many lessons learned through your ministries.

It is a book of my journey and some of the lessons I've learned along the way. I was on my way to a church business meeting when I saw a David Bridal sign while riding down Route 38 in Maple Shade, NJ which said David's Bridal dresses for all occasions. The Word dresses stood out in my mind. Although we continued down the highway, I began to see the letters

D.R.E.S.S.E.D. in my mind and by the time we arrived at the church, the acronym was embedded in me . . . Demonstrating Readiness Equipping Saints for Service Every Day.

DRESSED is defined - to treat or prepare in a certain way, to put in proper alignment, to put in order. It simply means to be prepared. Dressed in Righteousness, Dressed in Marriage, Dressed in Finance, Dressed in Business, Dressed in Relationships, Dressed to Serve, Dressed in Ministry. There is nothing that can defeat you, when you make Christ the center of your life. For Greater is He that is in you then he that is in the world. There is nothing that can take place today, that God has not been made aware of, and He has already made a means of escape just for you. For to me to live is Christ and to die is gain. (Philippians 1:21) This means that we no longer live according to the world system, we are dead and hidden in our Kinsman Redeemer, Christ Jesus. Either way we win because we are hidden in Christ.

*F*orward

As a bride is dressed and has prepared herself to meet her groom, this book is a personal directory for the true believer who is serious about meeting the soon coming King. The Bible has informed us as Christians to prepare and look forward to meet the King of Kings and Lord of Lords but we recognize that the enemy is sowing seeds of deceit by allowing many to disregard the most important element of Christian preparation. The writer is giving the reader a thought-provoking and uplifting view of important insights pertinent to soulwinning, and Godly living.

There are those who say that this preparation is "old school" and has nothing to do with today's Christian society but we are reminded of 2 Corinthians 4:4 KJV: "In whom the god of this world hath blinded the minds of them which believe not....... "

Anyone having doubt, or those who have been pondering concepts of concern in regards to why we Christians who are "the called-out ones" are encouraged to come out from among the "WORLD" in regards to the issue of Holy living.

This book having been written by such a powerfully inspired writer gives a clear view of the true believer's growth and lifestyle as one who has no desire to be swallowed up by the world to the extent that the unbeliever doesn't recognize or understand the difference between the world's standards and that of a person who is now born of God and works to save souls for the Kingdom of God.

Vernell Spann
M.A. Theology
B.A. Sociology/Psychology
A.A. ECD

# Preface

The goal of this book is to encourage you to walk with the Lord.

Life is not a problem to be solved, it is a mystery to live. You cannot solve life's problems. But you can be dressed (prepared) for every good work (2 Timothy 3:17). *"So, if anyone cleanses himself of what is unfit, he will be a vessel for honor: sanctified, useful to the Master, and prepared for every good work."* (2 Timothy 2:21). We wake up and use the bathroom and relieve ourselves, brush our teeth, shower, dry off, use lotion and deodorant and we begin the process of layering our clothes. This is what we need to do for our spiritual walk with God in the Kingdom. Wake up, be alert, pay attention, spend time in prayer, spend time listening for His voice, Accept Christ as our personal savior and Relieve ourselves of every weight and sin that doth so easily beset us. (Hebrews 12:1) Clean your mouth of any corrupt, filthy, and negative communication. Clean your mind of any stinky thinking. Be washed in the blood of the lamb through God's word. Then begin the process of putting on Christ by seeking Him daily through prayer and supplication making your request known unto God (Philippians 4:6). Studying the word of God (2 Timothy 2:15), applying that word in your daily life, For God's word is a lamp unto our feet and a light unto our pathway (Psalms 119:105). Therefore, as God's chosen people, Holy and dearly loved, clothe yourselves with compassion, kindness, humility, gentleness, and patience.

(Colossians 3:12). If we draw near to Christ, He will draw near to us. Then we can take on the characteristics of Christ which is the fruit of the Spirit. *"But the fruit of the Spirit is love, joy, peace, forbearance, kindness, goodness, faithfulness, gentleness and self-control. Against such things there is no law."* (Galatians 5:22-23) The fruit of the spirit is unified whole not independent characteristics. As we grow, all the characteristics of Christ will be manifested in our lives. Yet, like physical fruit needs time to grow, the fruit of the Spirit will not ripen in our lives overnight. Like a successful gardener must battle against weeds to enjoy the sweet fruit they desire, we must constantly work to rid our lives of the "weeds" of our old sin natures that want to choke out the work of the Spirit. You see the goal of all the children of God is for us to be like Christ. Let your root grow deep in the Lord, for the deeper the root, the sweeter the fruit.

D – Dedicated, Disciplined, Devoted and Determined

"Let your heart therefore be wholly devoted to the LORD our God, to walk in His statutes and to keep His commandments, as at this day."
1Kings 8:61

Dedication is the quality of being dedicated or committed to a task or purpose. It is making a quality decision to fully commit to a task or an assignment. In other words, "I'm all in." Let's take a look at the word of God. **2 Timothy 2:15** *says "Do your best to present yourself to God as one approved, a worker who does not need to be ashamed and who correctly handles the word of truth."* **In John 8:12,** *"When Jesus spoke again to the people, he said, "I am the light of the world, whoever follows me will never walk in darkness, but will have the light of life."* **Luke 9:62 Jesus replied**, "no one who puts a hand to the plow and looks back is not fit for the service in the Kingdom of God." Accepting Jesus into your life is a wonderful experience in and of itself but the privilege to carry out God's plan for our life is indescribable. It's Joy, Peace, and Contentment. It does not exempt us from trials and tribulations. It does not guarantee that we will live life without pains, disappointment, suffering, being misunderstood, sickness, etc.; but it does guarantee that we will live in Victory if we give Him our whole heart and walk-in total obedience to His word. In Psalms 84:11, *"For the Lord God is a sun and shield; the Lord bestows favor and honor; no good thing does He withhold from those whose walk is blameless."* In Job 1:1 There was a man in the land of Uz, whose name was Job; and that man was perfect and upright and one that feared God, and eschewed evil. At Satan's request, God allowed him to afflict Job, "you can touch all that he has but you can't take his life." He suffered much. The loss of his livestock, the loss of his servants, then a fire broke out and he lost his sheep and his servants, he lost all his camels to the Chaldeans and they killed his servants, He also lost his sons and daughters. You can imagine the degree of pain he was going through. The bible says that Job shaved his head and tore off his mantle and fell down and worshipped God. Verse 21 says *"Naked came I out of mothers' womb and naked shall I return. The Lord gave and the Lord has taken away; blessed be the name of the Lord."* Satan was not satisfied with the response of Job so he petitioned God again and ask God for permission to infect his skin that Job will curse God to His face. God told Satan to go ahead flesh and bones, but don't take his life. Satan attacked Job with boils from the sole of his foot to the crown of his head. Job took a piece of broken pottery (potsherd) and sat among the ashes. His suffering was great and I am sure seemly unbearable then his wife comes along and ask, are you still going to hold on to your integrity, why don't you just curse God and die. Some say she was used by the devil, others said that she agonized over his suffering. Regardless of the reason, Job in all his pain said to her, you speak as one of the foolish women speaks. Shall we receive good at the hand of God and not receive evil? But in all this Job did not curse God.

Take a few minutes and read Job chapters 1&2

What is your observation of the dedication and devotion of Job?

Think back over your life and the trials and tribulation you had to endure? How was your faith? Did you worship?

No doubt, Job was upset and in agony he cursed the day he was born, he longed for death, his grief was unbearable, but he knew of God's mighty power and His superiority even though Job got weary of life. Job held on to his peace and he knew that God would not be mocked. In chapter 13, the 15th verse Job said, *"Though He slay me, yet will I trust in Him: but I will maintain mine own ways before Him."* Job was saying regardless of what I am going through I will trust God. I Am All In. He was committed to follow God's plan for his life.

Can you say I Am All in? Take a few minutes and reflect on where you are now. What has your attention? What you give your attention and time to has your heart therefore your dedication.

This reminds me of a time my family lived in Crailsheim, Germany. My husband served in the United States Army for 24 years. We accompanied him on this tour of duty of Crailsheim, Germany. The origin of the "Horaffen" of Crailsheim, according to the story handed down, dates back to the siege of the city which took place in the winter of 1379-1380. In the course of the fighting among the towns in southern Germany, where "Free and Imperial Cities" who fought against sovereigns and nobility, there was a conflict between the allied imperial cities of Schwäbisch Hall, Rothenburg, and Dinkelsbühl and the Count of Hohenlohe. The allied enemies took their position under the walls of Crailsheim, so the tale goes, in order to take revenge for sufferings. The enemy soldiers lay siege to the city and tried to starve the citizens of Crailsheim in order to conquer them.

Before the enemies were able to achieve their purpose, however, the citizens of Crailsheim, after months of fighting, came up with a plan: the women gathered all the remaining flour, baked little pastries in the shape of a "Horaffen" (an open horn) and threw them over the wall. At the same time, the wife of the mayor courageously ascended the wall and revealed her bare buttocks to the enemies. Facing up to the abundance of bread and "bacon," the disheartened besiegers realized the hopelessness of their plan, and they withdrew on the Wednesday before Estomihi, 1380. Since this event, the citizens of Crailsheim are nicknamed "Horaffen."

Although the events of the besiege of the city in 1379-1380 are historically questionable, this legendary victory provides one of the reasons for the traditional City Celebration Day which has been celebrated now for 150 years on Wednesday, usually in February. On this day, the traditional "Horaffen" pastry is distributed to both children and the elderly in the city. We learned a great deal about dedication, determination and discipline during our stay. Crailsheim was determined to stand together as a community against the enemy and they were victorious. Our children had an opportunity to participate in the town yearly parade while they tell the story of their defeats and victories. Therefore, learning the importance of being all in.

My husband is a very disciplined man. Garland (my husband) took every assignment very serious and was exemplary at work and at home. However, during this time he had not accepted Christ as his personal savior. He grew up attending church, but had not made that personal commitment. He had some thoughts about the local church. He looked at people's behavior and their sometimes lack of dedication and their seemingly crooked walk on what he felt should be a straight path and felt that was not for him. My parents and my sister came to visit us one summer for a week's vacation. While in conversation my mother asked Garland why he had not given his life to Christ. She loved him and admired this discipline and dedication to the Army as well as to his family. He responded, "I see so many people that say they are Christians, but I see no fruit of it. No discipline, they say what they want, they do what they want and seem to be no conviction." My mother would respond "you must not look at others, this is a personal walk, you must follow Christ's example. He is the author and finisher of your faith." She prayed and believed that someday he would find joy in serving God. After my family left. It was sometime later not sure the exact time, however, Garland and I revisited the conversation he and my mother had. I told him that I believe God would save him and my entire household. His response was "I will not say I will never give my life to Christ, but I will say this if I do, I will not be a hypocrite." I will be all in. My husband gave his life to Christ, fully committed and dedicated to carry out what God has put in him in 1995. My mother never got the opportunity to see and experience the love of God that radiates through my husband. She died in 1993, but she believed that God would save him. Now retired working as the head trustee of our church. Dedicated, disciplined devoted and determined to carry out the work of the local church as it relates to the area of ministry as Head Trustee. He teaches us through his action how to be good stewards over what God gives us. He takes his position very serious. He often says, "not on my watch." Many times, we chuckle when he announces that he would like to see the members for a few minutes after service. Some have said, "When Trustee Kinard speaks everyone listens." His heart is wholly and completely devoted to the work of the Lord.

Is your heart fully wholly and completely devoted to what God has commissioned you to do?

Prayer:

Father in the name of Jesus, I thank You for giving me life, health and strength. I thank You for loving me so much that You gave your only begotten son to die on Calvary's cross just for me. I have given my heart to You, however, forgive my unbelief and lack of dedication at times. I now surrender all of me to Your will and to Your way. Please make me again another vessel. A vessel of honor meet for Your use and prepared for every good work. I now dedicate my life to the work of Kingdom building, body, soul and spirit. May I hear and do Your will in Jesus' name. Amen

Thought to Remember: *Whatever your hand findeth to do, do it with all of your might for there is no work, nor device, nor knowledge, nor wisdom, in the grave, whither thou go.* Ecclesiastes 9:10

Carolyn's personal and private lessons learned in my time in Prayer: April 28, 1993 7:46 am

My living room in Vicenza, Italy

Good Morning Holy Spirit.

I read St. Luke 10:16-21

"Whoever listens to you listens to me; whoever rejects you rejects me; but whoever rejects me rejects him who sent me."[17] The seventy-two returned with joy and said, "LORD, even the demons submit to us in your name."[18] He replied, "I saw Satan fall like lightning from heaven.[19] I have given you authority to trample on snakes and scorpions and to overcome all the power of the enemy; nothing will harm you.[20] However, do not rejoice that the spirits submit to you, but rejoice that your names are written in heaven."[21] At that time Jesus, full of joy through the Holy Spirit, said, "I praise you, Father, LORD of heaven and earth, because you have hidden these things from the wise and learned, and revealed them to little children. Yes, Father, for this is what you were pleased to do."

Chapter 02

R- Righteousness and Rest

Isaiah 32:17 &18 *And the work of righteousness shall be peace; and the effect of righteousness quietness and assurance forever. And my people shall dwell in a peaceable habitation, and in sure dwellings, and in quiet resting places;*

Righteousness is the perfect holiness of Christ. It is an essential attribute to the character of God; which means "One in right standing."

The commentary tells us that the law of Christ introduces a judgment or rule by which we must be governed, and the gospel of Christ is righteousness by which we must be saved; and, wherever the Spirit is poured out, both these dwells and remain as an everlasting righteousness. Peace and quietness. The peace here promised is of two kinds: — Only God can bring us true peace in this world. Jesus said, "Peace I leave with you; my peace I give you. I do not give to you as the world gives. Do not let your hearts be troubled and do not be afraid." (John 14:27).

[1.] Inward peace follows upon the indwelling of righteousness. Those of us that walk-in righteousness shall experience the blessed product of it. It is Peace in itself, and the effect of it is quietness and assurance forever, that is, a holy serenity and security of mind, by which the soul enjoys itself and enjoys the Most-High, and it is not in the power of this world to disturb it in those enjoyments. Note, Peace, and quietness, and everlasting assurance may be expected, and shall be found, in the way and work of righteousness. True satisfaction is to be had only in true religion, and there it is to be had without fail. Those are the quiet and peaceable lives that are spent in all godliness and honesty. First, Even the work of righteousness shall be peace. In the doing of our duty, we shall find an abundance of true pleasure, a present great reward of obedience in obedience. Though the work of righteousness may be toilsome and costly, and expose us to contempt, yet it is peace, such peace is sufficient to bear our charges. Secondly, the effect of righteousness shall be quietness and assurance, not only to the end of time, of our time, and in the end, but to the endless ages of eternity. Real holiness is real happiness now and shall be perfect happiness, that is, perfect holiness, forever.

[2.] Outward peace. It is a great mercy when those who by the grace of God have quiet and peaceable spirits from the providence of God which is made to dwell in quiet and peaceable habitations, not disturbed in their house or solemn assemblies. I have come to know the more we try to satisfy others and please others the more unsettled and disturbed we become. I don't care how pure your intentions are, even with the family the closer they are to us the more we feel their rejection. I am reminded of the recent conversation I had with one of my sons, I was attempting to suggest some ideas and options that we can offer his daughter, my granddaughter as a holiday treat. My intention was not to tell him what to do, nor was I suggesting that he did not know what to do. But somehow the conversation went in such a direction that I felt rejected. My perception was that my son thought I was just trying to be showy and in competition. That was the furthest thing from my mind, I experienced a temporary loss of outward peace. This rejection can lead to discord in the home. I became so vexed that I felt the need to repent and ask God to forgive me for not seeking Him first as to how to give my suggestions to my son or just keep silent and not suggest anything at all. I also asked God to restore my peace. Once I prayed, I called my son and ask for forgiveness if I was out of line. I only wanted to help to make her holiday special. My daughter helped me understand that it was possible that I was trying to impart my idea of what parenting should be, when in fact he has a different idea of what parenting looks like to him. I do find myself guilty of trying to protect and shield my children from any possible harm. Which is no longer my job with adult children. Everyone must go through their own wilderness experience. I must admit, at that moment, that I was done. Sometimes I feel that the things I've imparted in my children seem to have no significant value, notwithstanding they all know and have experienced God's grace and mercy in their life. I believe children should have a firm foundation. I tried to instill morals and values which stem from a foundation of Love and righteous living. It has little to do with money, but I felt that time invested in their lives would outweigh anything money can buy. However, now as adults, it is time to just trust what my husband and I have imparted in them. There are times where we will be disappointed, misunderstood and even sometimes a loss of outward peace, but Christ does not tell us to avoid these people who disrupt our outer peace. He also does not tell us to pretend that everything is fine. Instead, we are to continue to pray and share the love of God even at times it results in being stressful to us and it shakes our countenance. I will continue to love, minister, serve and reach out in humility.

Hebrews 4:1-16 REST

Therefore, since the promise of entering his rest still stands, let us be careful that none of you be found to have fallen short of it. For we also have had the good news proclaimed to us, just as they did; but the message they heard was of no value to them, because they did not share the faith of those who obeyed. Now we who have believed enter that rest, just as God has said, "So I declared on oath in my anger, 'They shall never enter my rest.'" "And yet his works have been finished since the creation of the world. For somewhere he has spoken about the seventh day in these words: "On the seventh day God rested from all his works." And again, in the passage above he says, "They shall never enter my rest." Therefore, since it still remains for some to enter that rest, and since those who formerly had the good news proclaimed to them did not go in because of their disobedience, God again set a certain day, calling it "Today." This he did when a long time later he spoke through David, as in the passage already quoted: "Today, if you hear his voice, do not harden your hearts."

For if Joshua had given them rest, God would not have spoken later about another day. There remains, then, a Sabbath-rest for the people of God; for anyone who enters God's rest also rests from their works, just as God did from his. Let us, therefore, make every effort to enter that rest, so that no one will perish by following their example of disobedience. For the word of God is alive and active. Sharper than any double-edged sword, it penetrates even to dividing soul and spirit, joints and marrow; it judges the thoughts and attitudes of the heart.

Nothing in all creation is hidden from God's sight. Everything is uncovered and laid bare before the eyes of him to whom we must give account. Therefore, since we have a great high priest who has ascended into heaven, Jesus the Son of God, let us hold firmly to the faith we profess. For we do not have a high priest who is unable to empathize with our weaknesses, but we have one who has been tempted in every way, just as we are—yet he did not sin. Let us then approach God's throne of grace with confidence, so that we may receive mercy and find grace to help us in our time of need.

Rest is walking by faith in God

Rest is having peace with God.

Rest is knowing and understanding that Christ's work was finished on the cross, therefore, we walk in the finished work of Christ, Jesus, through His grace and mercy.

Rest is freedom from a bondage-like spirit in the worship and service of God.

Rest is deliverance from the burden of legalistic practices we sometimes place people in church

Rest is freedom to worship in spirit and in truth.

Rest is enjoying the rest that God Himself enjoys.

Rest is _____

_____.

Fill in the blank.

What is rest to you?

Has there been times along your journey, when you have felt unrest?

What steps will you take to enter into His rest?

"Let us, therefore, make every effort to enter that rest, so that no one will perish by following their example of disobedience". Hebrews 4:11

Complete the scripture

"Let us, therefore, _____ _____ __ _____ to enter that rest, so that no one will _____ by following their example of _____."

Hebrews 4: _____

Father We thank You for the grace You have given us, the access to enter into Your rest. Let us be mindful to remain in right standing with You through obedience, righteousness whereby obtaining rest. In Jesus' name. Amen

Chapter 03

E – Eager and Encouraged

2 Corinthians 9:2

For I know your readiness, of which I boast about you to the Macedonians, namely, that Achaia has been prepared since last year, and your zeal has stirred up most of them

Colossians 3:23

Whatever you do, do your work heartily, as for the Lord rather than for men,

2 Timothy 2:15

Be diligent to present yourself approved to God as a workman who does not need to be ashamed, accurately handling the word of truth.

Romans 12:1

Therefore, I urge you, brethren, by the mercies of God, to present your bodies a living and holy sacrifice, acceptable to God, which is your spiritual service of worship.

1 Thessalonians 5:11 *Therefore encourage one another and build each other up, just as in fact you are doing.*

Hebrews 10:23-25 NIV *Let us hold unswervingly to the hope we profess, for he who promised is faithful. And let us consider how we may spur one another on toward love and good deeds, not giving up meeting together, as some are in the habit of doing, but encouraging one another—and all the more as you see the Day approaching.*

Let's define

Eagerness - enthusiasm to do or to have something;· **zeal · passion ·
earnestness · commitment**

Encouragement - the action of giving someone support, confidence, or
hope

When you have been given an assignment and you have full understanding
and direction it is easy to become eager and zealous. I enjoy studying God's
word, I enjoy sharing what I receive and learn from God's word. God has
allowed me countless opportunities to minister to people in different parts
of the world. I served as the Director of the women's ministry at our Gospel
Service in Italy, created and wrote the Monthly Newsletters, Encouraging
women (Women with Purpose). Our theme scripture was Exodus 9:16 *"And
in very deed for this cause have I raised thee up, for to shew in thee my power;
and that my name may be declared throughout all the earth.* I held in home
Bible Studies as the Lord led us.

My husband was given an assignment to relocate to Vicenza, Italy. We
moved to 58 Via Ancona, Torri Quantesolo, Italy. I was praying and doing
my daily devotion when I was led to shut in for a month. It was for a time
for Studying God's word, Praying and receiving instructions from the Lord
and taking care of my family. I did not understand it initially, however,
I know obedience is better than sacrifice. It was about the third week of
the shut in when I received a knock on the door. It was a lady that lived
on our block. She asked if she could talk with me, she said I was sent by
the unction and leading of the Holy Spirit. I did not know her, but I felt
peace and allowed her to come in. This sweet neighbor welcomed us to the
community. Then she began to tell me she was the Assistant Pastor's wife of

the Gospel Service on Base. And as we began to talk the Holy Spirit allowed me to encourage her and the power of God came in and she began crying out and praising the name of the Lord. It was an awesome experience to me. I had never received a welcome and an instant connection with anyone in this manner. Before her departure she asked if she could invite some other ladies to meet me. I said yes, and each week more and more women would show up at my door and before long about 30 women were coming into our home. This turned into a bible study. All of this was God's doing. I sought Him every morning to lead and guide me in the way He wanted me to go. I also said, "Father I did not start this lady's bible study group, You did. Help us to keep it pure and simple." God did just that. One morning in prayer, the spirit of the Lord spoke to me and said a lady will be coming to the door today. Greet her saying the following words, "Welcome Elect Woman of God." That afternoon it was a knock at the door. It was a different lady than the ones that had visited previously. I thought about the instructions I received earlier and I greeted the person at the door, by saying Welcome Elect Woman of God. She was and still is a precious young woman of God very special to me. After spending time with her, she told me she asked God to give her a sign that I was a woman of God by having me greet her as one of God's Elect. This all took place in 1993, and until this day this precious sister and I have remained close. Just like the spirit of God started the bible study, He ended it. Shortly after I began having dreams about a home going service. In this dream I saw the entire service and when I went to view the body it was my mother. I had this dream several times and I became deeply troubled by this dream and I would pray and rebuke the enemy, but the dream kept coming. This was peculiar because my mother was alive. She was a great leader of women, A pastor's wife, a devoted mother, a seamstress, an advocate for children, a musician and an anointed vocalist. She was strong and very courageous. Then I had another dream that I was in a relay race. I was running with all of my might and strength. My right hand was extended in front of me to receive the baton when I got close enough, the person in front of me was still running but looking back at me. I finally caught up with this person and when I touched the baton, I saw it was my mother. When I caught up to her, I took the baton and kept running with all my might. Little did I know that at that time my mother who was this great leader of women and Elect woman of God was about to transition. These two dreams troubled me deeply. I would pray, but I did not get an answer. Finally, one day I received a call from my sister, Sharon, and brother, Gary, that our mother was ill and I needed to come home. I asked my husband if he would get me out of here as soon as possible. I spent the last 30 days with my mother before her transition. She was an absolute Phenomenal Woman of God. God prepares us for every step of the Journey.

I returned to Italy. I was grateful for the dreams I had because it made her transition easier for me to handle. Evangelist Caroline Drumgoole, a close family friend and dear sister sent me photos by mail. Photos taken of my moms' Home Going Service. I cried and cried and cried and thought of all the lessons I learned through this Elect woman of God. How blessed I was to have such a virtuous woman as an example. That I came through the womb of a woman with such strength and courage. She was selfless and loving. I created a scrapbook and, at the end of it I understood why I had to Shut In, I understood why that precious neighbor had to knock on my door, I understood why it was necessary for the various women to show up at our home and why I needed to serve them through bible study and fellowship, I understood why a dear sister needed to be greeted in a specific way. So, Father, I thank You for the Holy Spirit that leads and guides us.

I became more eager to be of service to the Lord. However, sometimes in our eagerness and our zeal we can become over confident and self-assured. I Peter 5:8 The **devil**, as a roaring lion, walketh about, **seeking whom he may devour**. He goeth about as the lion, **seeking** for prey. The lion while hunting only roars when it springs. So, the **devil** is stealthy and does not give warning of his approach.

I must share this story. This happened during my shut in and months before I went back home to spend time with my mother prior to her transition.   One afternoon, feeling great and I can now say full of myself, I received a knock at the door it was a lady, a Jehovah Witness. She wanted to share her faith with me. Instead of welcoming her in to serve her. I did not receive her. I turned her away. It was not my first experience with talking to a Jehovah Witness, in the past I have sat down and I received insight to minister to their needs. I don't know why I turned her away but it did not sit well with me, because I knew that I was equipped and loving and kind enough to speak the truth in love. I knew that I was an ambassador for the Lord. I was a Christian which means Christ-like. Jesus would never have turned her way without ministering to her need. We must be instant in season and out of season. II Timothy 4:2 says *"Preach the word; be prepared in season and out of season; correct, rebuke and encourage--with great patience and careful instruction."* **Whether we feel like it or not we must continue to share God's word. Listen and understand,** if we do only what we feel inclined to do, some of us would never accomplish anything. Matthew 5:20 says, *"For I tell you that unless your righteousness surpasses that of the Pharisees and the teachers of the law, you will certainly not enter the kingdom of heaven."*

I received the following reprimand.

April 28, 1993 7:00 am (In the living room)

Before you accepted your call and received your ministry you had a family. Your willingness to forsake all was not in my perfect plan. If you love, truly love me (Christ Jesus) take care of your family and their needs, treat them as special as you do guest. Teach them the word, pray with them like you've done with the women and others who sought your counsel. Fulfill their wants and desires as unto the Lord. Once they know and understand what you know about me (Christ Jesus) my love, my forgiving power, my Wisdom, then and only then can you go forth without any reservation and with your family's total support. Let your family be your audience. They are special. They are my Gift to you and what you do with the gift will show me how much you appreciate it. He went on to say: Some of the problems and thoughts in your head comes from Satan. Vs 16 He hears me and he despises me and he also despises God. Carolyn, keep your thoughts pure, Resist those unclean thoughts. Thoughts that depress; oppress, criticize, put down and discourage, false accuse, angers, selfishness. Resist these thoughts. You have the ability. You have been given power and authority through the blood of Jesus Christ to tread on serpents' head and over all the powers of Satan and nothing, nothing, nothing shall by any means harm you. Do not boast in this power because it is not by your might, nor by your power but by the Spirit of God. That's why I used the Jehovah witness. You boasted in yourself instead of in me. You must remain humble, seek my face daily. Continue to ask for my direction. Now rejoice in the Lord, that is the only way you can rejoice without pride and boastfulness. Again, I say rejoice.

Father, thank You for Your kindness and mercy. Help me to keep my mind on You, and not get weary. Amen 0813

Oh! What a faithful Father.

Galatians 4:18

"It is fine to be zealous, provided the purpose is good, and to be so always, not just when I am with you."

NOTES

Make a list of things you are Eager to do for the Kingdom of God?

What are you doing to encourage others?

David encouraged himself in the LORD **His God. (1 Samuel 30:6)**

After fighting the Amalekites, David and his men returned to Ziklag to find that their wives and children had been taken captive by their enemies, and their homes burned.

There will be challenges and opportunities along your journey so Don't forget to encourage yourself!

Write an affirmation that will encourage you to remain eager to accomplish the work of the Lord.

Chapter 04

S– Submit and Study

James 4:7 - *"Submit yourselves, then, to God. Resist the devil, and he will flee from you".*

1 Peter 5:6 – "Humble yourselves therefore under the mighty hand of **God**, that he may exalt you in due time:

Jeremiah 17:10 - *"I the LORD search the heart and examine the mind, to reward each person according to their conduct, according to what their deeds deserve."*

"What causes fights and quarrels among you? Don't they come from your desires that battle within you? You desire but do not have, so you kill. You covet but you cannot get what you want, so you quarrel and fight. You do not have because you do not ask God. When you ask, you do not receive, because you ask with wrong motives, that you may spend what you get on your pleasures. You adulterous people, don't you know that friendship with the world means enmity against God? Therefore, anyone who chooses to be a friend of the world becomes an enemy of God. Or do you think Scripture says without reason that he jealously longs for the spirit he has caused to dwell in us? But he gives us more grace. That is why Scripture says: "God opposes the proud but shows favor to the humble." Submit yourselves, then, to God. Resist the devil, and he will flee from you. Come near to God and he will come near to you. Wash your hands, you sinners, and purify your hearts, you double-minded. Grieve, mourn and wail. Change your laughter to mourning and your joy to gloom. Humble yourselves before the Lord, and he will lift you up. Brothers and sisters, do not slander one another. Anyone who speaks against a brother or sister or judges them speaks against the law and judges it. When you judge the law, you are not keeping it, but sitting in judgment on it. There is only one Lawgiver and Judge, the one who is able to save and destroy. But you—who are you to judge your neighbor?
James 4:1-12 NIV

Many view the act of submission as a negative. I have noticed the word obey has been omitted or replaced in many marital ceremonies. I have spoken with women that say I can respect him, but I cannot obey him. But it is very important to understand the importance and the meaning of this word as it relates to our walk with God. We serve a God of order. To submit is to come under authority. This does not mean the husband is your boss, the Christian husband is your covering, he is to look out for your best interest, he is to love you like he loves his own body. We ask our children to submit or walk-in obedience so that we can protect them and lead them in the right path. This is why it's important for us to submit so that our heavenly Father can protect and provide and lead us in the way that most honor Him. It is our obligation to obey God. I know somethings the request seem strange and sometimes it doesn't seem to make much sense, but we must learn to lean on and obey God. Do you remember the story of Noah and the ark? God saw the wickedness of men in the earth, but Noah found grace in the eyes of God. Read the entire 6, 7 & 8 chapters. It will be manna for your soul. Here are a few verses and exerts of the story.

Genesis 6:8-14 But Noah found grace in the eyes of the LORD.

These are the generations of Noah: Noah was a just man and perfect in his generations, and Noah walked with God. And Noah had three sons, Shem, Ham, and Japheth.

The earth also was corrupt before God, and the earth was filled with violence.

And God looked upon the earth, and, behold, it was corrupt; for all flesh had corrupted his way upon the earth.

And God said unto Noah, the end of all flesh has come before me; for the earth is filled with violence through them; and, behold, I will destroy them with the earth.

Make thee an ark of gopher wood; rooms shalt thou make in the ark, and shalt pitch it within and without with pitch. He was given a strange request, you see no one had ever seen rain at that point in time. Can you imagine what the people thought and said amongst themselves about this old man building this huge boat when there was no ocean or lake around? But Noah obeyed and look what happened.

The 8th chapter of Genesis 1-14 **But God remembered Noah** and all the wild animals and the livestock that were with him in the ark, and he sent a wind over the earth, and the waters receded.

Now the springs of the deep and the floodgates of the heavens had been closed, and the rain had stopped falling from the sky.

The water receded steadily from the earth. At the end of the hundred and fifty (150) days the water had gone down, and on the seventeenth day of the seventh month, the ark came to rest on the mountains of Ararat.

The waters continued to recede until the tenth month, and on the first day of the tenth month, the tops of the mountains became visible.

After forty days Noah opened a window, he had made in the ark and sent out a raven, and it kept flying back and forth until the water had dried up from the earth.

Then he sent out a dove to see if the water had receded from the surface of the ground.

But the dove could find nowhere to perch because there was water over all the surface of the earth; so, it returned to Noah in the ark. He reached out his hand and took the dove and brought it back to himself in the ark.

He waited seven more days and again sent out the dove from the ark.

When the dove returned to him in the evening, there in its beak was a freshly plucked olive leaf! Then Noah knew that the water had receded from the earth.

He waited seven more days and sent the dove out again, but this time it did not return to him.

By the first day of the first month of Noah's six hundred and first year, the water had dried up from the earth. Noah then removed the covering from the ark and saw that the surface of the ground was dry.

By the twenty-seventh day of the second month the earth was completely dry.

The mountain of Ararat was a place of great hope and refuge for Noah. He had been floating around for five months. He seemed lost in a sea that had no end. Noah's obedience to God and his leadership had brought him into a place of isolation. At this moment he was on his own.

Noah knew that he had found favor in the eyes of God because he and his family were the only ones alive. Yet despite this, I can imagine to Noah, it seemed, he had been forgotten, or perhaps this is how he may have thought as he drifted on a sea going in no particular direction from one month to the next, hearing nothing from heaven.

God did not tell him how long he would be confined to the ark. God did not tell him when or how he would be released.   Noah was in a boat with a lot of stinky stuff. Many times, in our lives we find ourselves surrounded by stinky stuff going in no particular direction from month to month sometimes even from year to year. At times it can feel like there is no release, no end. The stinky stuff just keeps coming. Perhaps many would have been ready to conclude to themselves that God has forgotten them. Maybe even Noah possibly thought, "*how much longer, Lord, will You forget about me?*" All Noah had was the promise God gave him.

The first four words of the first verse. "But God remembered Noah." There have been times in my life were these four words brought comfort to me. But God remembered Carolyn.

The important and significant thing about this mountain is that Noah and his family did not climb Mt. Ararat. He and his family were taken to this mountain by God Himself. It was a place of safety and a place of refuge and a place of Divine Promise. If God had called Noah into the ark and shut him in, then it would be God who would open the door and lead him out. Trust and Obey. As a child growing up, there was an old hymn we use to sing in church:

 **TRUST AND OBEY written by John H. Sammis in 1887**

When we walk with the Lord in the light of His word what a glory He sheds on our way.

While we do His good will, he abides with us still, and with all who will trust and obey.

Trust and Obey for there's no other way to be happy in Jesus but to trust and obey.

Not a burden we bear, not a sorrow we share but our toil doth He richly repay;
Not a grief or a loss, not a frown or a cross, but is blessed if we trust and obey

Trust and Obey for there's no other way to be happy in Jesus but to trust and obey.

But can never prove the delights of his love until all on the altar we lay; for the favor he shows and the joy He bestows, are for them who will trust and obey.

Trust and Obey for there's no other way to be happy in Jesus than to trust and obey.

Then in fellowship sweet we will sit at his feet or we'll walk by his side in the way, what he says we will do, where he sends, we will go; never fear only trust and obey

Trust and Obey for there's no other way to be happy in Jesus but to trust and obey.

I am a witness that God will carry you through every situation if you learn to trust and obey.

I was in my daily devotion when I began to pen these words on January 16, 1994, at 9:50 am

STILL OBEY ME

When all your finances are gone and I say endure;
Still, obey Me.

When your health seems to fail and I say trust me;
Still, obey Me.

When all you speak from me seems to fall on deaf ears;
Still, obey Me.

When you desire to work and I say stay home;
Still, obey Me.

When education is deep within you and I say wait;
Still, obey Me.

When you desire to go out and shop and I say not;
Still, obey Me.

When you want to turn left and I say turn right;
Still, obey Me.

When you want to stop and I say go;
Still, obey Me.

When you want to sleep and I say rise;
Still, obey Me.

When you want to eat and I say fast;
Still, obey Me.

When you want to go and I say no;
Still, obey Me.

When you want to drive and I say walk
Still, obey Me.

Why? My child, it's because I know all about you. I created you and I set up the situations and circumstances in your life today in order to justify and quality you on tomorrow. Be still my child for your way is not my way neither are your thoughts my thoughts. Just remember I care for you and I know what's best for you. Obey me still because obedience is better than sacrifice. I Jehovah Jireh (your provider) Jehovah Nissi (Your banner), Jehovah Shalom (Your peace), Jehozabah (Your bestower), Jehubah (Your hiding place), Jehucal (Your ability), Jehozadak

(Your justification), Jemuel (Your light). I AM HE that holds the key to life eternal in My hands and the power to fulfill life in you.

Thank You, Father, for this writing and for the confirmation of Your word last night and Yes Lord, still in spite of everything I will obey You. Amen

1. Do you think it was easy for Noah to obey?

2. What would have happened if Noah hadn't obeyed God?

3. How did God reward Noah's obedience?

4. What are some things that you have been asked to do that was a little strange?

The way to get comfortable in your obedience to God is through studying His word.

2 Timothy 2:15 says "Do your best to present yourself to God as one approved, a worker who has no need to be ashamed, rightly handling the word of truth." When you spend time in prayer and in God's words there is an assurance and a guarantee that God will watch over His word. And it will not return void. It will accomplish everything that it was set out to do. When I pray and receive understanding I am compelled to obey. I find that His yoke is easy and his burden is light, (Matthew 11:30); however, when I walk in disobedience and neglect prayer and study of God's word. I lack understanding which makes my way hard. Good understanding gives favor: but the way of transgressors is hard. (Proverbs 13:15) Devote time in prayer, devote time studying God's word, and most of all, Trust and obey for there's no way to be happy in Jesus.

DRESSED IN MARRIAGE

DRESSED IN MINISTRY

DRESSED IN BUSINESS

DRESSED IN HUMILITY AND
OBEDIENCE

S – Spiritual Awareness and Sacrifice

Ephesians 6:12 *For we wrestle not against flesh and blood, but against principalities, against powers, against the rulers of the darkness of this world, against spiritual wickedness in high places.*

2 Corinthians 10:4-6 *The weapons we fight with are not the weapons of the world. On the contrary, they have divine power to demolish strongholds. We demolish arguments and every pretension that sets itself up against the knowledge of God, and we take captive every thought to make it obedient to Christ. And we will be ready to punish every act of disobedience, once your obedience is complete.*

(Romans 12:1 NKJV) *I beseech you therefore, brethren, by the mercies of God, that you present your bodies a living sacrifice, holy, acceptable to God, which is your reasonable service.*

There was no place in which the apostle Paul met with more opposition from false apostles than at Corinth; he had many enemies there. Let not any of the ministers of Christ think it strange if they meet with perils, not only from enemies, but from false brethren; for Paul himself did so. Though he was useful to all, yet there were those who did not like him, who envied him, and did all they could to undermine him, and lesson his interest and reputation. Therefore, he vindicates himself from their imputation, and arms the Corinthians against their insinuations. In this chapter the apostle, in a mild and humble manner, asserts the power of his preaching, and to punish offenders (2 Corinthians 10:1-6). He then proceeds to reason the case with the Corinthians, asserting his relation to Christ, and his authority as an apostle of Christ (2 Corinthians 10:7-11), and refuses to justify himself, or to act by such rules as the false teachers did, but according to the better rules he had fixed for himself (2 Corinthians 10:12 to the end).

Spiritual awareness can be a good thing or a bad thing, depending on the spirit in question and the motive of the person seeking the awareness.

42

Connection to evil spirits is not beneficial. Unfortunately, evil spirits often present themselves as beings of light and knowledge, and "even Satan disguises himself as an angel of light" Eve can testify to that. The spiritual awareness she was promised by the serpent do not benefit her. It causes her and Adam to disobey God.

Jesus was spiritually aware. John 2:24–25 But Jesus on this part did not entrust Himself to them, because He knew all people and needed no one to bear witness about man, for He Himself knew what was in man. He knew those that came against Him to try and entrap Him. In Acts 8:23 Peter as an Apostle of Jesus was given the ability to see the spiritual condition of Simon the sorcerer in Samaria: "I see that you are full of bitterness and captive to sin"

We too as believers should possess some Spiritual Awareness. For he has rescued us from the dominion of darkness and brought us into the Kingdom of the Son He loves. Colossians 1:13. We are in a spiritual battle every day. It is important to know that it is not against flesh and blood. Ephesians 6:12 *For we wrestle not against flesh and blood, but against principalities, against powers, against the rulers of the darkness of this world, against spiritual wickedness in high places.*

We must keep ourselves free from things that come to keep us from hearing from the Spirit of the Lord. It is important to set our affections on things above. Did you know your spirit can be altered by the things you say, the things you do, the company you keep and even the things you wear? Be cautious of the movies you watch, the conversations you find yourself in, the jewelry and apparel you wear. I Peter 5: 8-9 Be alert and of sober mind. Your enemy the devil prowls around like a roaring lion looking for someone to devour. Resist him, standing firm in the faith, because you know that the family of believers throughout the world is undergoing the same kind of sufferings.

In 1981 I lived in the small village of Buedingen, Germany. Pregnant with our first child, I joined a Women's Christian Fellowship group. I was attending their weekly bible studies. There is a Military Exercise Campaign called Reforger (from the return of forces to Germany) it was an annual exercise and campaign conducted, during the Cold War, by NATO. The exercise was intended to ensure that NATO had the ability to quickly deploy forces to West Germany in the event of a conflict with the Warsaw Pact. This particular year every one of the lady's husbands in our Women's Fellowship group was sent out on the exercise except my husband. I thought, "This is odd." I would later find out that this was part of God's plan. As a teenager, I enjoyed horror movies, was interested in spiritualism, Ouija boards, and movies like "The Exorcist" and "Texas Chain Saw Massacre." My mother warned me against such movies. They were dangerous and unholy. That I was giving a foot hole for the devil. However, as a teenager, I thought I knew what was best for me. I said to myself it was just entertainment. It was just a game or just a movie. I believed Isaiah 54:17 *"No weapon formed against you shall prosper, and every tongue which rises against you in judgment You shall condemn. This is the heritage of the servants of the LORD, and their righteousness is from Me,"* Says the LORD. I also believed Luke 10:19 *"Behold, I give you the authority to trample on serpents and scorpions, and over all the power of the enemy, and nothing shall by any means hurt you."* I was young and foolish and should have stood on the scripture in Matthew 4:7 Jesus said to him, *"It is written again, 'You shall not tempt the Lord thy God."* We should never put God to a test. Unknowingly I was putting God to a test. I felt like I could not be tempted or harmed by anything the devil would throw at me. I protested the fact I was saved. Our heavenly Father is, The Most-High God. Whatever you give your attention to, you invite into your life. While young in the things of God. I was attending this Christian Women's group. As I forestated the men had gone out on Exercise Reforger. One of the leaders of the group suggested that since the husbands were out of town that we have the study group in her home. It was closer so we would not have to travel too far in the evening. It was actually within walking distance to my apartment. The ladies agreed and we begin going to her apartment. Initially, it seemed to be good. I was enjoying the study and fellowship. One evening during the prayer this woman said that the Lord was instructing her to invite the ladies to stay overnight and shut in for a couple of nights. Everyone was invited to stay except me because my husband was still at home. How many of you know that God will make a means of escape for you? 1 Corinthians 10:13 says, *"There hath no temptation taken you but such as is common to man: but God is faithful, who will not suffer you to be tempted above that ye are able; but will with the temptation also make a way to escape, that ye may be able to bear it."* At the time I did not realize that I would soon need that escape. The women decided to remain in her home, but I left and went home. The next morning, I went to work. I worked in another village about 20 – 25 minutes away. I was beginning to feel uneasy. I did not understand why, so I disregarded it and finished work. I got off about 5:00 and on my way home. I was on a narrow highway and an eighteen-wheeler was in the lane coming in my direction, we were coming around a curve on the high part of a mountain and he was coming so fast I just knew he was going to hit me. I began praying aloud and for what seemed like five minutes. I closed my eyes because I just knew I was going to be hit and I thought I was going to die because, the impact would have forced me off this mountain. But when I opened my eyes, I was still here, I was still on the road and when I looked in my rearview mirror, I saw the truck was still moving down the mountain. I began to cry and praise the Lord for protecting me and saving me. I arrived home and that uneasiness returned. I did not understand it, so I again disregarded it. When you find uneasiness in your spirit stop and began to pray and get in God's word. It may be that God is trying to get your attention. But I disregarded it. It was time to go to the Women's Fellowship meeting and the uneasiness got stronger, the closer I got to house the more anxious I was becoming. Philippians 4:6 says *"Do not be anxious about anything, but in every situation, by prayer and petition, with thanksgiving, present your requests to God."* However, at the same time, I also felt I was being drawn in and felt I had to attend. I finally arrived there. When I entered the home, I looked at the faces of the ladies and their faces seemed troubled and fixed. Now I am uncomfortable, but can't seem to go back to the door and leave. The prayer began and the woman leading the group began to say, "Carolyn I saw you in the spirit today that you were on your way home from work and I saw an eighteen-wheeler coming towards you. I began to pray and Lord intervened." So, I said to myself, "this woman must be a child of God, how else would she have known that." Then she started speaking in an unknown tongue, passed out on the floor in a trance. At that moment, I begin to recall my life in my mind. My life flashed before me. I begin to remember how my mother and the other mothers of Zion would pray on the altar for their children. I could hear my mother praying. You see, I had experienced the move of God on my life and the life of others through their prayers. My flashing thoughts were suddenly interrupted when this woman sat up on the floor in Indian style with bloodshot eyes looking directly at me and said, "Carolyn Kinard, (she called my whole name) a woman is going to come to the door, if you let her in, I will kill her (the life of the woman who was leading the bible study)" Shortly after that, there was a knock at the door. Fearful, but I went to the door, and sure enough, there was a woman at the door. She asked if everything was okay. I heard noises. I reply, "Yes everything is just fine." She said, "Are you sure, I am a nurse. Is everything okay? Again, my reply was yes, everything was just fine. Once the door was close, my heart began to fear, then I remembered the scripture in 2 Timothy 1:7 *For God did not give us a spirit of timidity (of cowardice, of craven and cringing and fawning fear), but [He has given us a spirit] of power and of love and of calm and well-balanced mind and discipline and self-control. Mark 11:22-24 And Jesus answered them, "Have faith in God. Truly, I say to you, whoever says to this mountain, 'Be taken up and thrown into the sea,' and does not doubt in his heart, but believes that what he says will come to pass, it will be done for him. Therefore, I tell you, whatever you ask in prayer, believe that you have received it, and it will be yours.*

Luke 1:37 For nothing will be impossible with God."

I realized that I was under spiritual attack. I began to call on The Most-High God, the Great IAM, that is all powerful, all Knowing, all sufficient.

In my mind I saw my mother standing before me crying out to God. The demons in this woman began to rise up again with sounds and groaning and she appeared to get darker in complexion and her eyes were even more red than they were before. With everything in me I began to plead the blood of Jesus. I cried out to God like I had never before. I began to rebuke every unclean spirit. I prayed over the women that were there. She began to laugh loud and say, "You have come face to face with the devil, and you did not even know it." I was under spiritual attack. I was in spiritual warfare praying and fighting not just for me but also for the women that were there. I cried out to the Lord with all that was in me. **Psalm 18:6** *In my distress I called upon the **Lord,** and **cried unto my** God: **he heard my voice** out of his temple, and **my cry** came before **him,** even into his ears.* We serve a living Savior; we serve a God that is loving and doesn't treat us like we treat Him. Thank You, Father. I began casting out the vial and unclean spirits. Rebuking and Casting out demons, Rebuking and Casting out demons. Crying out to the Most-High for deliverance. God heard my cry and delivered us. Luke

10:19 says *"Behold, I give unto you power to tread on serpents and scorpions, and over all the power of the enemy: and nothing shall by any means hurt you"*. The last thing I heard from the demon was, "If you tell anyone, you will die. If you tell, you will die." I continued to pray until God sent peace. I looked around at the other ladies to ensure they were okay. I then grabbed my coat and left. When I got to my apartment, I went straight to the living room and fell on my knees, repenting for thinking it was okay to watch all of those demonic movies and toying with things and ideas that dishonored our God. I was gripped with fear. The spirit of the Lord led me to Revelation 3:15- 16

"I know thy works, that thou art neither cold nor hot: I would thou wert cold or hot. So then because thou art lukewarm, and neither cold nor hot, I will spew (vomit) thee out of my mouth."

I realized how I had dishonored God, I was straddling the fence and it made Him sick on His stomach to the point of vomiting. It grieved me to think that I felt my practices were okay. I love the Lord and gave my life to Him at a young age. I thought this was just entertainment. I repented and made a choice that day that I will rather be hot than cold. I decided to be all in. Does that mean I have not made mistakes along the way? No! But now thank God my appetite has changed. My appetite is for the presence of God.

Psalm 16:11 *says, "You will make known to me the path of life; In Your presence is fullness of joy; In Your right hand there are pleasures forever."* That is just what the Lord did for me and I am truly grateful. I kept the experience to myself for a while until one Sunday morning while visiting my home church in Camden, NJ. I was asked to greet the people and share a few words to encourage the people. As I began to speak, the experience I had began to spill out. Mind you, it was told to me if I tell of this experience I would die. I was hesitant, but the more I spoke the freer I became. This took place almost 40 years ago and I am still here. Hallelujah! Living for Jesus. Sensitive in spiritual things. A warrior for the Lord. Fighting the good fight of faith. Leaning and depending on the Lord in every area of my life. Hungry for the presence of the Most-High God. *" For I am not ashamed of **the gospel** of Christ: for it is the power of God unto salvation to everyone that believeth; to the Jew first, and also to the Greek."* Romans 1:16 For I know who I am and whom I belong.

"I am crucified with Christ: nevertheless, I live; yet not I, but Christ liveth in me: and the life which I now live in the flesh I live by the faith of the Son of God, who loved me, and gave himself for me. I do not frustrate the grace of God: for if righteousness come by the law, then Christ is dead in vain." Galatians 2:20-21

Lay aside every weight and sin that does so easily beset us. Confess your sins to God.

A prayer of Repentance

Heavenly Father, we come to You asking for forgiveness. I have made a mess of my life and need You. When I think I am right, I'm wrong and when I think I'm wrong I am right. I no longer want to live a life of uncertainty. I am asking that You come into my heart and live in me. For I am a sinner and I acknowledge my transgressions. I believe that You sent Your Son, Christ Jesus, to die for the remission of my sins and I know that He loves and cares for me, because Your Word tells me so. And Christ sits on the right side of You, Father, making intercession for me. Forgive me of my sins and cleanse me from all unrighteousness. Please come into my heart Lord Jesus. Thank You for hearing my prayer. I believe, I confessed and now I receive. Thank You, Lord for salvation in Jesus' name Amen.

A prayer of Deliverance and Restoration:

Father, I thank You for Your redeeming power, Your restoration power, Your deliverance power, and Your forgiving power. I pray now for all who knowingly and unknowingly are living in bondage. I speak deliverance, restoration, and peace now over your life. Satan, the Lord rebuke you. The blood of Jesus is against you. I bind every hindering spirit, every demonic spirit that blinds the hearts and minds of men, women, boys and girls. Satan through the blood of Jesus your power is rendered powerless in Jesus' name. I pray for the power of the Holy Ghost to open blinded eyes, reunite hearts and minds with our Heavenly Father. I pray for truth in the inward parts of man. I pray for a peace that passes all understanding to guard your hearts and minds in Christ Jesus. Thank You, Father for changing our appetite and thirst. For our appetite is for your presence. I thank you now Father for answering this prayer in Jesus name, Amen.

"Now may the God of hope fill you with all joy and peace in believing, so that you will abound in hope by the power of the Holy Spirit." Romans 15:13

Spend some time in your word and tell the Lord just how much you love Him and thankful for His presence in your life. God inhabits the Praises of His People. God wants to be with us...Jesus is evident of that. *"But thou art holy, O thou that inhabits the praises of Israel."* Psalms 22:3

Chapter 06

E – Enter In

Psalms 1 *"Blessed is the one who does not walk in step with the wicked or stand in the way that sinners take or sit in the company of mockers, but whose delight is in the law of the LORD, and who meditates on His Law Day and Night. That person is like a tree planted by streams of water, which yields its fruit in season and whose leaf does not wither— whatever they do prospers."*

Psalm 100 *"Make a joyful noise unto the LORD, all ye lands. Serve the LORD with gladness: come before his presence with singing. Know ye that the LORD he is God: it is he that hath made us, and not we ourselves; we are his people, and the sheep of his pasture. Enter into his gates with thanksgiving, and into his courts with praise: be thankful unto him, and bless his name. For the LORD is good; his mercy is everlasting; and his truth endureth to all generations."*

Hebrews 4:1 *"Therefore, while the promise of entering his rest still stands, let us fear lest any of you should seem to have failed to reach it."*

Deuteronomy 31:6 *"Be strong and courageous. Do not fear or be in dread of them, for it is the LORD your God who goes with you. He will not leave you or forsake you."*

Webster dictionary defines Enter as to make a beginning; to go upon the land for the purpose of taking possession; to cause to be received or admitted. It takes a hunger for the presence of God. That hunger will give you a pursuit to go after the things of God. David had a hunger for the presence of God. Oh, David was far from being perfect, but he loved God and continued to have a hunger and longing to be in the presence of God.

Psalm 63:1-11
O God, you are my God; early will I seek you: my soul thirsts for you, my flesh longs for you in a dry and thirsty land...

Moses was another person who hungered for the presence of God. He understood that without God, he could do nothing. Moses had a speech impediment and did not think he could accomplish the task to tell "Pharaoh to let my people go." He wondered how would others know that God found favor with him?

"If Your presence does not go with us, do not lead us up from here. For how then can it be known that I have found favor in Your sight, I and Your people? Is it not by Your going with us, so that we, I and Your people, may be distinguished from all the other people who are upon the face of the earth?" Exodus 33:15-16

We serve an intentional God. God did not heal Moses of his speech impediment. He raised up Aaron to accompany him on the journey. If God has a task for you, He will provide you with everything you need to accomplish that task, an Aaron to help you on your way, so don't be afraid to Enter in.

In all thy way acknowledge Him and He will direct your path. I think about the four seasons that we have here in the North-East portion of the United States and how it is necessary to prepare to enter into each one. We are currently in the Winter season. It is cold and sometimes snowy. It has a tendency to dry out your skin. So, I find that it takes a little heavier lotion or cream for my skin to remain hydrated. I have to cover my head with a hat to protect me from catching a cold. I must layer my clothing with sweaters, scarves, and heavier pants and skirts to protect myself against the

blistering winds, I sometimes need boots rather than sneakers to protect my feet. Sometimes while I am in the house getting dressed to go outside, I begin to get hot, but I understand this is temporary because I am about to enter into the inclement weather. And likewise, in the summer months, those same clothes that you needed in the Winter months are of no use to you. But with all of the preparation, it does not keep me from entering into the season. The season is going to come whether we are ready or not. Many times, we tell ourselves that, "I'm not ready to do this or to do that." So, we ignore the call because of fear or lack of confidence, or lack of preparation which will keep you from your destiny. I have found that if God takes you to an opportunity, He will bring you through it. But you must be willing to enter in. Don't Procrastinate! What are you waiting for? Procrastination can cause you to miss out on the promises of God for your life. Now is better than never, yesterday you missed your chance and tomorrow is not promised, so try it today! Try it today! Enter in with thanksgiving, enter in with praise, enter in rejoicing, enter in with the full assurance that you will finish strong. New career, enter in! New relationship, enter in! New ministry, enter in! God will never put more on you than you are able to bear. I Corinthians 10:13

"There hath no temptation taken you but such as is common to man: but God is faithful, who will not suffer you to be tempted above that ye are able; but will with the temptation also make a way to escape, that ye may be able to bear it."
The time is now so, Enter In!

What are the dangers of Procrastination?

What are your fears or reservations?

For God _____ _____ given us the spirit of_____; but of _____, and of _____, and of a sound _____. I Timothy 1:7

Father, we thank You for granting us access to Your kingdom. Help us to be bold soldiers, for You. Help us to Enter into the gates with thanksgiving. Enter into our journey with You in faith and courage to finish the race that has been set before us in Jesus' name Amen.

Chapter 07

D- Dedicated and Duty Bound to walk into the destiny that God has prepared and promised you.

Deuteronomy 10:12

"Now, Israel, what does the LORD your God require from you, but to fear the LORD your God, to walk in all His ways and love Him, and to serve the LORD your God with all your heart and with all your soul,

Deuteronomy 6:5

"You shall love the LORD your God with all your heart and with all your soul and with all your might."

Joshua 22:5

"Only be very careful to observe the commandment and the law which Moses the servant of the LORD commanded you, to love the LORD your God and walk in all His ways and keep His commandments and hold fast to Him and serve Him with all your heart and with all your soul."

Micah 6:8

"He has told you, O man, what is good; And what does the LORD require of you but to do justice, to love kindness, and to walk humbly with your God?"

Ecclesiastes 12:13

"Now all has been heard; here is the conclusion of the matter: Fear God and keep his commandments, for this is the duty of all mankind."

It is in Matthew 22:37, where Jesus states that the duty of man is to love God with all his heart, soul, and mind, and to equally love other human beings. Man was created and therefore duty bound to worship God in truth and in all honesty and to do to others as he would like done to him.

We have a duty to uphold. A responsibility as a Christian to be ambassadors for Christ. A duty to serve God by serving others. John 9:4 As long as it is day, we must do the works of him who sent me. Night is coming, when no one can work.

Dedication is a vital step that when committed to a task or purpose allows us to see the results of what was rebuilt. Far too many people trust **God** for the strength to restore a relationship or career, only to take it back once in frustration they find the work to be hard. God never promised us that things in this life would be easy, but He did promise never to leave us alone and that He would take us through every situation. Moses went to Mount Sinai in Exodus 31 and 32 God was telling Moses about the tabernacle workers that had been chosen. Then the instructions on keeping the Sabbath Holy and at the end of His communing with Moses, God gave him two tablets of testimony written of stone. When all of the people saw that Moses took so long in coming from the mountain, they took it upon themselves and gathered together unto Aaron asking him to let them make a god that will go before them. *"We don't know what happened to Moses."* *So, Aaron told them to take off the gold earrings, your wives, your sons and daughters are wearing and bring them to me. So that is what they did. Aaron received them and fashioned them with a tool and made them into an idol cast in the shape of a calf. Then Aaron built an altar in the front of the calf and told the people tomorrow there will be a festival to the Lord. So, the next day the people rose early and sacrificed burnt offerings and fellowship offerings. Afterward, they sat down to eat and drink and got up to indulge in revelry. God told Moses to go down, because your people whom you brought up out of Egypt, have become corrupt. They have been quick to turn away from what I commanded them and have made themselves an idol cast in the shape of a calf. They have bowed down to it and sacrificed to it and have said, "These are your gods, Israel, who brought you up out of Egypt. These people are stiff-necked. Now leave me alone so that my anger may burn against them and that I may destroy them. Then I will make you into a great nation." But Moses sought the favor of God. The Lord relented and did not bring on his people the disaster he had threatened.*

However, when Moses returned from the mountain with the two tablets in his hands. They were inscribed on both sides, front and back. These tablets were the work of God, the words were the writing of God, engraved on the tablets. When Moses approached the camp and saw the calf and all of the dancing, he became angry and threw the tablets down breaking them into pieces. Then he took the calf that the people had made and burned it in the fire and grounded it to powder, scattered it on the water and made the Israelites drink it. Then he went to his right-hand man, Aaron, asking what did you let these people do to you, that caused you to lead them in a great sin?

Can you imagine the frustration that Moses felt? Moses a man devoted and dedicated to the work of the Lord. I can imagine that the thoughts crossed his mind, how he saw a burning bush and realized he was on holy ground and the need to remove his shoes, then chosen to deliver the people out of Egypt and the process he went through, not feeling adequate enough because of his challenges of speech. Then to arrive in Egypt and the Pharaoh refusing the message from the Lord and how Moses watched the Lord bring plague after plague after plague unto the Egyptians and until Pharaoh finally released them. Then to bring them to the Red Sea watch the Lord open the sea with the rod God had given him. Seeing 600,000 men, women, and children make it safely across and then watching Pharaoh and his army drown in the same sea that they walked across. The Lord in all of His mercy brought them out of the land of Egypt, a place of oppression. The God that provided Manna from heaven, led them by fire at night and clouds during the day.

Receiving instructions directly from the mouth of God through Moses. I believe Moses was sadly disappointed and angry when he went back to the Lord and said, "oh, what a great sin these people have committed!" they have made themselves gods of gold. But now, please forgive their sin – but if not, then blot me out of the book you have written." Even though Moses did not have anything to do with the gold calf. The fact he was so angry he threw down the precious tablets he was just given. He felt bad. Now because of their sin, they will receive a plague. The Lord told Moses when the time comes for me to punish, I will punish them that sinned against me and blot out of my book. And the Lord struck the people with a plague because of what they did with the calf Aaron had made.

Moses' frustration caused him to break the tablet of instruction that was meant for the people. How many times have you attempted to do all you can for someone only to find that they decided to do something else contrary to what instructions were given to them? There are times even as parents you deposit the word of God, the wisdom that you have obtained, and the love you have in your children, and then they turn their back on your teachings and choose another path of life. Just like Moses pleaded for the children of Israel, you have pleaded for your children. God's ways are higher than our ways. His thoughts are higher than our thoughts. I am a witness He hears our plea and our supplication. He does not always answer in the way we want Him to. But His answers are always perfect and always for our good. Moses asked the children of Israel Who is on the Lord's side. We must ask ourselves and all that God has allowed to accompany us on this journey Who is on the Lords' side? There was still a promise of the land with milk and honey. Who is on the Lord's side?

Thank You, kind Father, for not consuming us in our sin. Thank You for Your forgiveness.

We must be faithful unto death in order to receive the crown of life. The bible tells us when you put your hands to the plow don't look back. If you do, you are not fit for the Kingdom. We must give God our all. Let His word make His abode in you, reside in you and, live in you. Set up residence in you. If you draw nigh to Him, He will draw nigh unto you.

Let no one deceive you. If God be for you, He is more than the world against you. I had a dream many years ago while living in Germany. I was captured and taken from my home to a chopping block in the village square of our community. Guards had my children with them and one of the guards put my hand on the chopping block and looked at my children and told them if they would deny Christ, he will let me go. I cried out NO, never deny Christ. The guard cut off one of my fingers, I saw the children crying and I repeated never deny Christ, never, never deny Christ. The guard chopped off another finger. I continued to cried out don't you dare deny Christ. The guards will kill me either way if they can. But God is our true deliverer. I woke up in a cold sweat. I shared my dream with my children. It became my mission to introduce my children to Christ at a young age. And continue to live a life before them that they may see my good works and glorify our Father which is in heaven. And with all that is within me, I will fight the good fight of faith. Trust in the Lord with all my heart and lean not to my own understanding. In all my ways acknowledge Him (Christ) and He will direct my path. I was encouraged and admonished to teach them to love their neighbors as themselves. More than thirty years have passed and God has given us a wonderful and glorious relationship. We still meet daily by phone early in the morning to continue to encourage each other in the things of God. I so treasure this time spent with them. We hold one another accountable and encourage each other of the responsibility of dedicating our lives to God while pursuing our destiny. The destiny that has been ordained from the beginning. You see Christ is the way, the truth and the light. No one can come to the Father except by His son. We have a duty to uphold, teach your children, teach your grandchildren, teach your nieces and nephews, teach all who are in your path. Teach with all meekness and wisdom. Watch your speech for the weapons of our warfare are not carnal, but they are mighty through God to the pulling down of strongholds. The lack of devotion is a stronghold, all disobedience is sin; therefore, a stronghold. We must fight, for there is a war going on. But we have the victory through Jesus Christ our Lord.

FOOD FOR THOUGHT

D - *Daily spend time in communion with the Lord.*

E – *Encouraging one another daily*

D – *Deny yourself of worldly lust in pursuit of the presence of God.*

I – *Insight- We pray that the God of our Lord Jesus Christ, the Father of glory, may give you the Spirit of wisdom and of revelation in the knowledge of Him.*

C – *Casting all of your cares upon Him, for He cares for you.*

A – *Acknowledging and Accepting the will of God for your life.*

T – *Teaching and admonishing others about the love of Christ.*

E – *Exalting and praise God for His mighty works.*

D – *Discernment - But examine everything carefully; hold fast to that which is good; abstain from every form of evil.*

DUTY BOUND

"I speak after the manner of men because of the infirmity of your flesh: for as ye have yielded your members servants to uncleanness and to iniquity unto iniquity; even so now yield your members servant to righteousness unto holiness." Romans 6:19

"Let us hear the conclusion of the whole matter: Fear God, and keep His commandments: for this is the whole duty of man. For God shall bring every work into judgment, with every secret thing, whether it be good, or whether it be evil." Ecclesiastes 12:13-14

PURPOSED AND PREPARED FOR

D – DECLARE - *For I know the plans I have for you, declares the LORD, plans for welfare and not for evil, to give you a future and a hope. Jeremiah 29:11*

E - ENDURE - *Blessed is the man who walks not in the counsel of the wicked, nor stands in the way of sinners, nor sits in the seat of scoffers; but his delight is in the law of the LORD, and on his law, he meditates day and night. He is like a tree planted by streams of water that yields its fruit in its season, and its leaf does not wither. In all that he does, he prospers. The wicked are not so, but are like chaff that the wind drives away. Therefore, the wicked will not stand in the judgment, nor sinners in the congregation of the righteous; ...*

S -STEADFAST IN THE LOVE OF GOD- *The LORD will fulfill his purpose for me; your steadfast love, O LORD, endures forever. Do not forsake the work of your hands. Psalm 138:8*

T – TELL OF HIS GOODNESS -*And I heard a loud voice from the throne saying, "Behold, the dwelling place of God is with man. He will dwell with them, and they will be his people, and God himself will be with them as their God. He will wipe away every tear from their eyes, and death shall be no more, neither shall there be mourning, nor crying, nor pain anymore, for the former things have passed away." Revelation 21:3-4*

I – INSTRUCTION - *Listen to advice and accept instruction, that you may gain wisdom in the future. Proverbs 19:20*

N – NOTHING LACKING - *And let steadfastness have its full effect, that you may be perfect and complete, lacking in nothing. James 1:4*

Y – YOU - *You are my hammer and weapon of war: with you I break nations in pieces; with you I destroy kingdoms; with you I break in pieces the horse and his rider; with you I break in pieces the chariot and the charioteer; with you I break in pieces man and woman; with you I break in pieces the old man and the youth; with you I break in pieces the young man and the young woman; with you I break in pieces the shepherd and his flock; with you I break in pieces the farmer and his team; with you I break in pieces governors and commanders. Jeremiah 51:20-23*

For _____ has not _____ us for wrath, but _____ _____
_____ _____ our Lord Jesus Christ.   1 Thessalonians 5:9

Father, we thank You for Your love and mercy towards us. As we dedicate and devote our lives to You Guide us, for we need Your guidance, yes, we need Your guidance, we can do nothing without Your guidance. G U I D A N CE (GOD U AND I DANCE). We need that intimacy as we continue on this journey. If You lead us, we will follow and if You hold our hands we won't go astray. Thank You for the grace and mercy that will continue to follow us all of the days of our life in Jesus' name Amen.

Chapter 08

Are you D.R.E.S.S.E.D. for life interruptions?

WHAT? Are you D.R.E.S.S.E.D. for an interruption? WHAT? WHERE IS THIS COMING FROM? Are you prepared for the beginning of sorrow? WHAT ARE YOU SAYING? There are times when everything seems to be going smoothly and without warning, BOOM! KAPOW! CRASH! your normal routine, your current flow, the road along your journey has just been interrupted. It could be a sudden life change, a loved one dies, an unexplainable critical illness, an employment upset, a broken friendship, an unexpected tax audit, your church doors have closed. You are barred from visiting your elderly parents. You are unable to be with your wife that is about to deliver your child. I am writing this book at that very time. The entire country has suddenly been invaded by an invisible virus. This interruption has affected all of us. The Coronavirus (Covid-19) pandemic is identified as the cause of an outbreak of respiratory illness. A **type of common virus that can infect your nose**, **sinuses**, or **upper throat**. They can spread much like cold viruses. Almost everyone gets a coronavirus infection at least once in their life, most likely as a young child. COVID-19 symptoms include cough, fever, shortness of breath, muscle aches, sore throat, unexplained loss of taste or smell, diarrhea, and headache and some have no systems at all. The mystery is you can't see it. It is airborne and it is said that it can live on metal in addition to and other materials and because we can't see it, we have been quarantined in our homes. If we need to leave our homes, we must have a mask covering our noses and mouth and latex gloves. Most children are now doing online schooling, parents and a great part of the working community are working from home. Most corporate and small businesses have been affected and there are many closures and layoffs. In the midst of writing this book unemployment lines have increased. More than 26 million people have filed in the past five weeks. It is predicted that 20 million people will be unemployed. Disinfectants, toilet paper, paper towels, water have become scarce. To date globally, there have been more than 3 million confirmed affected people with the coronavirus and more than 217,000 deaths and these numbers are growing daily and far from over because they say there is no found cure. Why am I bringing this up? There are so many things that men are saying. We must know what Our Father in heaven has said in his word. This is where we will find the truth. Read and study with understanding Matthews 24:1-7

"And Jesus went out, and departed from the temple: and his disciples came to him for to shew him the buildings of the temple. And Jesus said unto them, see ye not all these things? verily I say unto you, there shall not be left here one stone upon another, that shall not be thrown down. And as he sat upon the mount of Olives, the disciples came unto him privately, saying, tell us, when shall these things be? and what shall be the sign of thy coming, and of the end of the world? And Jesus answered and said unto them, take heed that no man deceives you. For many shall come in my name, saying, I am Christ; and shall deceive many. And ye shall hear of wars and rumors of wars: see that ye be not troubled: for all these things must come to pass, but the end is not yet. For nation shall rise against nation, and kingdom against kingdom: and there shall be famines, and pestilences, and earthquakes, in divers' places."

Are we experiencing pestilences, earthquakes and famines in the earth? In 2020 alone thus far just to name a few: Haddon Heights, New Jersey (WPVI) -- A powerful storm left a trail of destruction in Ocean County, New Jersey on Tuesday afternoon April 28, 2020. Taal Volcano Eruption spewed a massive cloud of ash, Australia's deadly bushfires, Brown New Zealand Glaciers was an after mass of the Aussie bushfire, Vegetation in the Himalayas Glaciers are melting, Floods in Dubai, Flood in Indonesia, Storms in America's deep South, Now Coronavirus – hitting just about every area on the earth.

Matthews 24:8-27, *"All these are the beginning of sorrows. Then shall they deliver you up to be afflicted, and shall kill you: and ye shall be hated of all nations for my name's sake. And then shall many be offended, and shall betray one another, and shall hate one another. And many false prophets shall rise, and shall deceive many. And because iniquity shall abound, the love of many shall wax cold. But he that shall endure unto the end, the same shall be saved. And this gospel of the kingdom shall be preached in all the world for a witness unto all nations; and then shall the end come. When ye therefore shall see the abomination of desolation, spoken of by Daniel the prophet, stand in the holy place, (whoso read this, let him understand:) Then let them which be in Judaea flee into the mountains: Let him which is on the housetop not come down to take anything out of his house: Neither let him which is in the field return back to take his clothes. And woe unto them that are with child, and to them that give suck in those days! But pray ye that your flight be not in the winter, neither on the sabbath day: For then shall be great tribulation, such as was not since the beginning of the world to this time, no, nor ever shall be. And except those days should be shortened, there should no flesh be saved: but for the elect's sake those days shall be shortened. Then if any man shall say unto you, Lo, here is Christ, or there; believe it not. For there shall arise false Christs, and false prophets, and shall shew great signs and wonders; insomuch that, if it were possible, they shall deceive the very elect. Behold, I have told you before. Wherefore if they shall say unto you, Behold, he is in the desert; go not forth: behold, he is in the secret chambers; believe it not. For as the lightning cometh out of the east, and shineth even unto the west; so shall also the coming of the Son of man be".*

There is a warning to the children of The Most-High God, the creator of heaven and earth. A warning to the pastors and leaders of our churches. We must study the word of God, search the scriptures and prepare ye the way of the Lord. Our responsibilities as believers in Christ is to prepare and direct people directly to our Heavenly Father through the redemptive blood of Christ and we do this by the leading of the Holy Spirit and by lifting up the name of Christ the Son of the Living God. Not just vain talk, but in our lives. Living out the word and allowing the word of God to take root in our heart that we do not sin against God. That we crucify our sinful nature and arm ourselves in His righteousness, through obedience and submission to the word of the Lord.

Other scriptures to reference of warnings. What are these scriptures speaking to you?

Ezekiel 33

Jeremiah10

Jeremiah 23

Jeremiah 24

Prayer: Father have mercy on us according to Your loving kindness and the multitude of Your tender mercies. Please forgive us and blot out our transgressions, wash us with hyssop make us white as snow. Forgive our ignorance, and lack of knowledge, our slow-fulness, our lawlessness, our rebellious behavior, our laziness, our faithlessness. We know your word says in Hosea 4:6 *"My people are destroyed for lack of knowledge: because thou hast rejected knowledge, I will also reject thee, that thou shalt be no priest to me: seeing thou hast forgotten the law of thy God, I will also forget thy children."*

It was announced and explained that it came out of China and the first positive case came from Washington State. I was in the midst of preparing for a baby shower in Newark, NJ. When this interruption came. I had five events scheduled from March to July. Every event has been postponed or rescheduled. My living room and sunroom filled with supplies that I had prepared to use at the events. Sitting around looking at the boxes and flowers, arches, easels, and the list goes on. Initially I did not want to move anything I thought this will pass and will not last too long. One event was scheduled on March 15, 2020. We had been planning for this event since November 2019. We worked so diligently preparing for this event shopping for the right materials and specific crystals, unique boxes for display purpose and pricing ghost furniture (clear acrylic) pieces that would accent the display. Gold crowns varying in sizes and the list goes on, after all of that we still were not sure if we would be able to work this event. So much money and time had gone into this event. We were so excited both the clients and myself about it. In the midst of the excitement about the March 13th, we were interrupted by the news of the Coronavirus. The clients were determined not to cancel. So, we took every precaution with ensuring everything was clean and the clients asked that no one attend that had any flu symptoms. The clients decided they were going to have the event. So, we set up this event. It was a great success. To God be the Glory.

I had 5 additional events lined up for the next couple of months and as time moved on, more people were getting sick and dying, we were now quarantined in our homes. Clients were forced to reschedule or postpone their engagement to later in the year and even some rescheduled for 2021. In my mind, I thought this would be over soon so I left everything I had prepared and lined up for my events as they were. My granddaughter came from New York and stayed with us from March 22 to May 3. We began assisting her with homeschooling, completing assignments, having morning meetings and getting her acclimated with Zoom on the computer. Things were changing every day and in every way. My son's job was essential and therefore, needed to work outside the home. Doctor's appointments that were lined up for me, I canceled because hospitals were being inundated with sick patients from the Coronavirus. We cannot go out without a mask, we are also advised not to touch our face, keeping six-foot apart practicing safe distancing. We were notified that we were now in a Pandemic. 164 days have gone by, many people have become anxious and frustrated and many have decided to violate the order of staying at home. I must honestly admit I have had total peace being home. I thank God for His grace, mercy, and love. I have not utilized my time as efficiently as I hoped however, I thank God for this time being at home. Boy oh boy, His love keeps me secure, His love keeps me safe, His love keeps me whole, His love keeps me in perfect peace when my mind is stayed on Him. I decided to put things back in my warehouse and make notes so that once the quarantine has been lifted, we will be ready to go again. However, I began to think about what if things don't go back to what we know as normal. I began to think about the things that have been good about the quarantine. A time to reconnect with family members in the household. Time to check on neighbors to see if they need anything, Time to wave to neighbors passing by, Time to sit at the table together to enjoy your meals with a conversation; more time allotted for prayer and bible study. Time to declutter the things that were just in the way, both naturally and spiritually. The world is talking about a new normal. Father, in the name of Jesus, I want a new spiritual normal, walking with discernment, walking in wisdom, walking in righteousness, walking in clarity, walking with purpose, making good decisions, walking in Holiness, Walking by Faith, Walking in Love, Full of the Holy Ghost, Full of Dunamis power to stand against the wiles of the devil, and fully armed so that I don't fall prey to the tricks and traps that man and or the enemy may set for me.

Living a simple and pure life helps to prepare you for interruptions that may come your way. Wearing loose garments (not holding on to traditions of man, legalistic practices, worldly lust, pride, etc.) but holding on to the horns of the altar allows us to continue our walk in the Lord as we face challenges in our life, dying daily to the things of the world, learning to lean on Christ in every situation and in all things, not for all things, but in all things give thanks unto the Lord. I thank God for His word. There will be a new normal after this. There will be victory after this. For the devil is defeated and God is exalted.

Father continue to Break up the fallow grounds in our lives help us to know the truth of Your word and walk in that truth and live in that truth. Give us the knowledge and understanding we need to be bold soldiers in the earth. 2 Timothy 3:16-17 says, *"All Scripture is God-breathed and is useful for instruction, for conviction, for correction, and for training in righteousness, so that the servant of God may be complete, fully equipped for every good work."* Change the lives of your people that we may accomplish the work that we have been D.R.E.S.S.E.D. to do. We thank You now for Your grace that unmerited favor, that covers our ignorance. That same Grace will not cover or excuse our willful and repeated sin against our Father. For those that don't know you in the pardon of their sin we pray that You will draw them as we continue to lift you up according to Romans 10:9-13, "that if you confess with your mouth Jesus as Lord, and believe in your heart that God raised Him from the dead, you will be saved; for with the heart a person believes, resulting in righteousness, and with the mouth he confesses, resulting in salvation." For the Scripture also says in, "WHOEVER BELIEVES IN HIM WILL NOT BE DISAPPOINTED." For there is no distinction between Jew and Greek; for the same Lord is Lord of all, abounding in riches for all who call on Him; for "WHOEVER WILL CALL ON THE NAME OF THE LORD WILL BE SAVED."

I would like to invite you to give your life to Christ, you can pray this prayer:

Father I confess with my mouth my sin before You and realize that there is no salvation apart from You. I am ASKING for Your forgiveness of my sins and ASKING that You will come into my life and save me. I BELIEVE in my heart that You Most High, raised Christ Jesus from the dead. I CONFESS that Christ Jesus is the Son of The Most-High, The Great I AM and He has redeemed my life. I thank You for Your love and saving me and setting me free. In Jesus' name Amen.

Write your confession of Faith:

According to scripture if you truly repent and ask the Father to forgive you and you believe in your heart you are saved. However, it doesn't stop there. Get in the word of God and study and Pray and study more and pray for understanding. Find a bible believing church that will teach you the word of God. Not religion but the truth of God's word. God is looking for a real relationship with you. "All those the Father gives me will come to me, and whoever comes to me I will never drive away." John 6:37. Study baptism and Ask to be baptized. Don't forget to Praise and Worship our Father for all that He has done.

"In the same way, I tell you, there is rejoicing in the presence of the angels of God over one sinner who repents." Luke 15:10.

Welcome brother, sister to the body of Christ!

References

Matthew Henry Commentary

NIV Bible

KJV Bible

Covid 19 information – Internet

Crisis listed from different areas in the world - Internet

Aristotle Quote - Internet